The Essentials of Catholicism

Everything you need to know in under 100 pages

MICHAEL TIGUE

Contact the Author

Michael Tigue
mtigue@web4uonline.com
888-254-3213

Table of Contents

Contents

Why the Essentials?

We learn a lot of stuff....just not the essential stuff.

Many critiques of Catholicism would be correct if Catholicism were what most of us think it to be. But, if we got down to the essential components of Catholicism and let the other more decorative components fit in where they belong, the entire picture would make more sense. The truth is that Catholicism *is* everything we hope and feel it should be. But, we need to uncover those basic, good and valuable truths first.

Catholics tend to have gathered a lot of data on things that are not essential to being Catholic and at the same time have never nailed down the truly essential doctrines.

For example, many Catholics can list most of the seven deadly sins but can't identify the five precepts of the Church. The five precepts of the Church are the five required minimum actions for being Catholic and the seven deadly sins are helpful memorization device to help us avoid temptation. Knowledge of the seven deadly sins is not required to keep one's baptismal Promises, but intentionally failing to do one of the precepts of the Church is a grave matter.

Some people think they can't eat a meal without saying grace, yet they might easily find a reason to miss Sunday Mass. It would be much better to eat meals without saying grace than to skip Sunday Mass. One is required, the other is optional.

6

Many Catholics can produce at least one fancy latin name for something found in the Church (thurible, vestibule, chalice, etc.) but can't explain the 6 major Covenants of salvation history covered in the Bible. To understand Jesus offering of a new and everlasting Covenant, one benefits greatly from knowing the five Covenants before it. One benefits very little from knowing that the sprinkler used during Easter season is called an aspergillum. It is not that these peripherals are not helpful or good. It is just that we need to cover the basics first, for our sake and for the sake of our Church's reputation.

We know great stories of incorrupt saints but don't know the four essential elements of a valid Marriage. We've been asked to write a report on our Confirmation Saint, but we've never been taught how to share the Basic Gospel Message.

There are plenty of books on latin names and saint's lives. This book starts and ends with the basics in less than 100 pages.

Many Catechisms have covered all of these basics inside their pages. But, their length and depth is too broad for the average user. *The Essentials of Catholicism* aims to put all of the essentials in your hands in a quick, readable format.

In the review process for this book, many pointed out that their favorite facts and figures were missing. However, I felt they were missing the point. This book had to be short and simple so that it would be used. Writing 400 pages of which zero are read is not nearly as effective as 100 pages read well or read twice. Or, worse yet, writing 400 pages of which only the non-essential pages are read would only perpetuate the very problem this book aims to fix; that we know a lot of Catholic stuff; just not the essential teachings.

So, instead of complaining about the state of affairs, I offer this book as a solution, to help you and anyone you know, quickly beef up on the essentials of Catholicism. There is a lot left out of course. But, this is my summary, of what a Catholic in 2014 should learn and learn quickly.

The Basic Gospel Message

The Message with its own Power

It all begins with the Basic Gospel Message. Some say the book should begin with the creation story and God's omnipotence…however, I was afraid you'd get bored with all that just like you get bored reading the Book of Genesis. I figure if you picked up a book that says "The Essentials of Catholicism" right on the cover, that you've already given God a chance to exist and that you figure He's worth learning about.

The Gospel Message is absolutely essential. It is the most essential element of the 9 elements and yet many Catholics do not know it. However, unlike other "facts" of Catholicism, the Basic Gospel Message is not just something you know. It is something you experience. The Basic Gospel Message is not just something you read or hear but something that comes off the page and into your life. In fact, it is not a "thing". It is a "person". The very proclamation of the Gospel has power (Kerygma). Something about these facts, when preached, brings about the power and presence of God. God does something when these words are proclaimed. This message contains within it an actual Godly power. It is not a normal story or a fairy tale.

9

We must receive a gift or an anointing to believe what is contained in this message. We cannot believe or accept this message on our own. It is not, fortunately, a matter of will alone, but a matter of grace. The gifted nature of the Basic Gospel Message brings us relief both as the hearer and as the preacher. When we preach this message we do not have to worry about being eloquent or wise, for the message itself testifies to itself. As the listener we don't have to worry about not believing because belief is a gift. Faith is a gift.

People often agree with me when I say that we first have to have a relationship with Jesus before we can grasp the many concepts of Catholicism. But then they ask, "How do you make someone else know Jesus?" "How do you cause it to happen?" I answer that I truly do not know how the Holy Spirit does it on the inside of us. But, I know you have to proclaim the message and you have to invite the listener to respond. As for precisely what and how the Holy Spirit makes the truth ring in our ears and verify it in our hearts....I don't know "how" He does that. I know there is free will and that a person can say no to the testimony of the Spirit. I also know the preacher can botch the proclamation or taint it by his ideas and attitude and that sometimes perhaps the Spirit protects the listeners from false teaching. But, despite the mystery of how the gift of faith is given, it is an essential component of Catholicism to know, receive, and then proclaim to others the Basic Gospel Message. In fact, almost nothing of Catholicism, especially the moral teachings, make much sense apart from the Basic Gospel Message.

So, what is the Basic Gospel Message? There are some key points you need to cover when preaching the Basic Gospel Message. The below 5 "b" words can help you remember those five major components.

10

1. Big – God is **Big** and good and created us good to be close with him as our Father.

2. Bummer – Generations before us sinned and we have sinned, which is a **Bummer** because it separates us from God and has brought sin and death into the world

3. Bridge – God, out of love for us, paid for the debts of our sin, which is death, by becoming man and dying on the cross. Jesus' sacrifice to the Father of death on the cross restores us to grace with the Father. In this way, Jesus becomes a **Bridge** from the kingdom of darkness to the kingdom of light. His Resurrection demonstrates that He has conquered both death and sin. We can take this Bridge if we choose

 4. Believe – We are called to **Believe** that this is true and Repent from our sins. Repenting means turning from Satan and sin and believing in Jesus Christ as the only path or Bridge to salvation

The Gospel message involves asking those listening if they would like to turn from sin and Satan and believe in Jesus Christ as Lord and receive His offering of salvation. You can ask the listeners to respond in various ways such as raising their hand, coming forward, or speaking words of acceptance out loud. But, you should at least ask them to respond to the invitation privately. The Gospel message does require an invitation to respond. Too many people have heard parts of this message and never been directly asked to repent and believe.

5. Behave – While we do not "earn" our way into heaven, being part of the kingdom of light involves following and obeying the commandments. By Faith and Baptism we enter into the kingdom of light, which is also joining a family. There is a basic code of conduct for members of this family, and therefore we still have to **behave**.

Sharing the Gospel Message

The Gospel message can be shared in large gatherings or one on one. It does not have to be shared in any particular way but the five major components, especially the first four, need to be shared. Part 4 has two parts, the repenting and believing. A lot of people like to skip the repenting part, but you just can't skip it. Think of John the Baptist and all the repenting he preached before Jesus. John the Baptist's whole life is a strong example of the importance of repenting before encountering Jesus.

Preaching the Gospel can be done at any time, but you should be prepared for those listening to respond emotionally. Satan doesn't take well to this message either, so visible signs of people being freed from darkness might also be seen. After you share the Gospel with someone, you should follow up with him/her when reasonably possible. The OCIA or RCIA program at your local parish is the organized method for bringing people into the Church. You might want to invite people to attend these sessions after you share the Basic Gospel Message.

Note: If you ever end up teaching OCIA, RCIA, or Sunday school, you really need to start with and once and awhile come back to the Basic Gospel Message. No one gets tired of hearing this message. I've heard it a lot of times and it is always powerful. Who doesn't want to hear that God loves them, that God gave his life for them, that their debts have been paid, and that new and eternal life is freely offered?

Besides the eternal benefits, I love hearing this message because it reminds me that God loves me now and that I can know and experience Jesus love and healing now, right now, on earth. St. Theresa of Avila said, "All the way to heaven is heaven itself."

To be true to my word, I have to ask you the reader, to re-read the Five B's above and make a decision for yourself if you'd like to repent from your sins and turn to Jesus as your savior. This is not a mental exercise. This is a choice you make in your soul about your soul and for your soul. You are in need of a savior. You cannot do it on your own. Your own efforts have only proven your need of a savior. Fortunately that savior exists in the person of Jesus. Tell him you are sorry for your sins and that you'd like to receive him into your life now. Tell him that you'd like him to be Lord of your life and that you surrender your life to him.

Questions

Have you ever been some where the Gospel message was preached? Were you asked to respond out loud or in a visible manner?

Have you ever had to share the Gospel message? Can you describe your experience?

Have you associated this with Protestant groups instead of Catholic groups?

Have you ever had a bad experience with the Gospel message being presented (too forceful, too demanding, etc.)

When and where do you think the Gospel message could be preached more in normal Catholic experiences? (Mass, OCIA class, Confirmation class, retreats, etc?)

Can you share a good experience of preaching or responding to the Basic Gospel Message?

What can you do to make sure Catholics preach and respond to the basic Gospel message more often?

Apostolic Succession
and Church Structure

Apostolic Succession is the concept that the original Apostles laid hands on their successors and ordained them to continue the Apostolic Ministry. All of the revelation that the Apostles received from Jesus is called the "Deposit of Faith". The deposit of faith was handed on from one generation of Apostles to the next. This continued passing on of the Deposit of Faith to the Apostle's successors and their successors is called Apostolic Succession. The succession has continued to the current day. We call the current successors of the Apostles "Bishops" and every Catholic Bishop can trace his succession back to one of the first Apostles. Never in the history of the Catholic Church have the Bishops in union with the Pope ever officially taught doctrine outside of the deposit of faith. The Deposit of Faith cannot be added to or subtracted from. Now, some elements not in the Deposit if Faith, such as when to celebrate St. Patrick's Day, can change and be moved around because they were not part of the original Deposit of Faith. But, the substantial dogmas and doctrines of the faith have not and cannot be changed. Only the Eastern Orthodox Church and the Catholic Church make claims to Apostolic Succession and have a valid line of Bishops. Only the Orthodox and Catholic Churches have all

15

seven sacraments and the original full content of the deposit of faith as their major faith tenants. There are a few minor disagreements between Catholics and Orthodox on the role of the Bishop of Rome, the pope. But in many major ways, the faiths are the same.

Most non-Catholic Christian denominations have at some point in their history added to or taken away from the original Deposit of Faith. In most cases, they have subtracted from the Deposit of Faith. They have broken from the Apostolic Succession and now offer a summary of doctrines, that while substantial and good, are missing elements from the original Deposit of Faith. For this reason, it makes a lot of logical sense to be Catholic.

Popular Piety

However, the contents of the Deposit of Faith are doctrines of belief and not necessarily the same thing as "popular piety", which is the way that the church members pray or worship. It can be the case then that Catholics, even though they have the full Deposit of Faith in doctrine, may, in their popular piety, take on actions or behaviors somewhat outside the Deposit of Faith. In addition, Protestants, not having the full Deposit of Faith, can still be moved by the Spirit to minister in powerful and meaningful ways. In this way, sometimes it may be more attractive on some ministry levels to join a Protestant Church over the Catholic Church. While this can be understandable on one level…one should also be compelled to examine on an intellectual level the contents of a religion's doctrine and compare it to the ancient and historical apostolic Deposit of Faith. Once presented with the historical continuity of the Deposit of Faith, one is often compelled, on an intellectual level, to become Catholic or remain Catholic.

It then becomes the responsibility of those who are compelled to be or stay Catholic to be open to the gifts of the Holy Spirit to help make the Catholic Church both doctrinally and spiritually fulfilling. Once convicted of the truth of Apostolic Succession, Catholics should work to make sure their Church is as welcoming and warm as it can be on a human level to help support and encourage a deeper look at its historical and doctrinal tradition. While the doctrinal accuracy is preserved by Apostolic Tradition and Papal Infallibility, the feeling, vibe, and pastoral aspects of the Catholic Church are in many ways dependent on her members' openness to the promptings and anointing's of the Holy Spirit. The Catholic Church is blessed by the accuracy of doctrine provided by Apostolic Succession, but she needs all members to contribute to her mission of outreach and evangelization. It is better to stay in the Catholic Church and help her than it is to leave her in protest.

On the point of protest, and the Protestant Reformation, it is worth noting that many of the original complaints by the Reformers were complaints against popular piety and not against the Deposit of Faith. Some of the complaints against popular piety were well founded and needed to be addressed. In some cases, the original reformers were not trying to create a new religion with a different set of doctrines but rather trying to reform the only Christian Faith that existed at the time, the Catholic Faith. In some cases, the followers of the reformers were the leaders in offering new or different doctrines or removing some doctrines from their core beliefs. In these cases, when the Deposit of Faith was altered, those believers had to officially leave their membership in the Catholic Church because the original Deposit of Faith cannot be altered.

After hundreds of years, many people are simply born into a Protestant or a Catholic family and grow up learning many false things about each other's religion. It is important to seek out the contents of the original Deposit of Faith, research Apostolic

Tradition and the current doctrinal teachings of the various Christian groups. I believe the Catholic Church's current and unchanged doctrines will speak for themselves. As for popular piety and pastoral execution, I have already shared how easily there can be room for improvement. However, this is not a point of challenge unique to the Catholic Church. Any religion and even any organization suffer from the frail behaviors of its members. However, a Christian organization, because it accepts the concept of original sin, should not be surprised that her members at times, do   fail.

Papal Infallibility

You have learned that Bishops are successors of the Apostles. The Bishop of Rome has since the time of Peter been the "Pope" or head Bishop. The Pope has a special gift called "Papal Infallibility" which means something different than most suspect it to believe. It does not mean the current Pope can predict sporting event outcomes or declare a new member to the Holy Trinity. He cannot decide Mary is part of the Trinity or that there are really nine sacraments. He cannot, as stated before, add to or take away from the original Deposit of Faith. He can only, when teaching officially as the Pope, teach and explain the Deposit of Faith. Throughout all history, there is no record of a Pope breaking from the Apostolic Tradition and the Deposit of Faith. In fact, on the issue of women ordination, it is sometimes the Pope's response that he has no authority or example from Tradition to give him any indication that he can act differently on this issue. In addition, even if one were able to view the soul of a previous Pope and judge him to be very unholy, one could not find an example of that pope officially teaching outside the Deposit of Faith. Even if his actions were publically opposed to the moral requirements of the Church, his official teaching never wavered. This again is a distinction between a Church member's actions and the official teaching of the Deposit of Faith. We should be Catholic because of the Deposit of Faith and not because its members are currently acting holy or not. After all, aren't we some of those members?

Papal infallibility is gift that offers us certainty about the contents of the Deposit of Faith. Without Papal Infallibility and Apostolic Succession, Catholics would be very free to alter the Deposit of Faith. Their religion would splinter into an uncountable number of variations. Many lower church protestant denominations suffer from this reality. Without any assurance that any one member is preserving the core beliefs, the beliefs are free to be altered by any one new teacher or preacher.

All this is to say that Apostolic Succession and Papal Infallibility should be looked at as guiding gifts and not limiting statutes. It should also be noted that Catholics are free to theologize inside the boundaries set by the Deposit of Faith. However, these boundaries are often wider than outsiders may recognize. For example, it is part of the Deposit of Faith that Jesus is both God and Man. He is both. The teaching is not one or the other, but both. This means that as a Catholic, you could write a book or give a long meditation on Jesus as Man. You would not in any way be violating Catholic Teaching. You could also write a book entirely about his divinity. You would only error if you stepped outside the boundaries and declared that he was no longer man or no longer God. At that point you would be leaving the confines of the Apostolic Tradition and would need to reconsider your conclusions or reconsider your membership in the Church. Many issues have wide boundary markers and Catholics are free to ponder and question inside those boundaries.

Priests, Deacons, Cardinals, Nuns etc.

We covered Popes and Bishops in the above sections. Priests are helpers to the Bishop. They carry out the role of the Bishop in partiality. They serve their Bishop by offering the sacraments of Confession, Baptism, Anointing of the Sick, Marriage, and Eucharist under normal circumstances. In some circumstances they offer the Sacrament of Confirmation. Deacons serve at their local parish and server the priests and members of the Parish. Deacons can offer the Sacrament of Baptism.

Nuns, Brothers, Sisters, and Monks, are names for the members of a Religious Order. While often used to portray the Catholic Church, religious orders are not essential components of the Deposit of Faith. They are however, a very practical grouping of individual Catholics who seek to commit themselves to life together and ministry and prayer of a certain kind. There are thousands of religious orders that devote their energies to tens of thousands of religious and service oriented tasks. They have been extremely helpful and instrumental in proclaiming the Gospel Message to the ends of the earth. Religious Orders need sacraments as well and for this reason, it is possible to be both a brother in a Religious Order and an ordained priest. A priest in a religious order can also be made a Bishop of a Diocese or Archdiocese. Nuns and sisters are female members of religious orders. Common religious order names are Dominicans, Franciscans, Benedictines, Sisters of Charity, etc.

Cardinals are usually Bishops but not necessarily. They are special helpers to the Pope and they participate in the election process of a

20

new Pope. They are not another step or part of the Sacrament of Holy Orders. (more on this in the Sacraments section)

Mary and Saints

The Church structure does not only consist of those on earth, but also those members who have gone before us and who are now in heaven.

It is a common misconception that Catholics worship Mary. It has never been nor will be part of Catholic doctrine that Mary is a deity that is to be worshipped. In fact, it is easiest to understand Mary by thinking of her on the human level. After all, she is human. On earth, most people seem to agree that is a good idea to ask other people to pray for them. We often receive prayer requests from friends when they are sick or someone in their family is sick. In times of real desperation we seem to ask anyone and everyone to pray for us. Catholics and non-Catholic Christians alike seem to think the more praying the better. We also seem to have a sense that someone whom we perceive to be holy is someone who might be able to get their prayers through to God more easily. Some people just seem to have a gift for their prayers being answered. And, in a time of need, we run to these people. Mary and the Saints are a lot like these "holy" people we turn to on earth. In fact, they are exactly like these "holy " people in that they are a) human and b) holy and close to God. Mary and the Saints, however, are perfectly holy and perfectly close to God. So, if you think your grandma or pastor has powerful prayers…you should try asking the Saints to pray for and with you too!

I think one of the main reasons Mary seems to pop up over and over again in the lives of Catholics is really quite a practical reason.

I think Catholics just seem to find on a very pragmatic level that getting Mary involved in their prayer petitions just seems to work. In the same way those on earth with a gift of preaching or a gift of healing seem to be in popular demand, so too are Mary and the Saints in popular demand. They are good at praying and so we ask them to pray for us.

The only real matter of faith to accept when it comes to Saints is believing that death is not a boundary. If you asked your 90 year old grandmother to pray for you and then one year later she passed away, you don't have to stop asking her to pray for you just because she died. Saints are simply deceased members of our Church family that have been officially recognized by the Church to be in heaven. However, it doesn't mean they are the only ones in heaven. They are just officially recognized and recommended prayer helpers. Think of the list of Saints and Mary as the Church's recommended list of preferred intercessors. If I were to ask you to name the 10 holiest people you know that I could talk to for prayer and advice, you could probably make a list. Well, the Church over the centuries has been compiling a pretty amazing list. And Mary, over time, seems to be a Saint who has every spiritual gift and who is very, very helpful in our prayer life. After all, she knows Jesus pretty well.

But, it is also worth pointing out that you don't have to ask the Saints for help to be Catholic. If the saints are a tough topic for you, don't worry about it for now. You can still be Catholic. Some topics are deal breakers like Jesus' divinity. But, personal devotions to saints are not a deal breaker. On the other hand, don't be alarmed if you find a Saint or two popping up in your life and trying to help you.

Questions

Have you heard about Apostolic Succession before?

What struck you the most from this section?

Which part of this chapter do you think most people don't understand very well?

Does this section change your views on anything in the Catholic Church?

Have you had any practical and positive experiences from asking Mary or other Saints to pray for you?

Do you know stories of Mary and/or Saints helping someone else in a real way?

Did you know it was possible to be Catholic and not have a big personal devotion to the Saints?

Covenants in Scripture

and their relationship to each other

To be in a Covenant means to be in a relationship. Covenants are like contracts; only they are deeper. In a contract, things are exchanged for other things or for money. In a covenant, people are exchanged and shared as people and for people. In marriage, the husband and wife give their entire person to each other. They hold nothing back.

Adam and Eve (couple)

God was in a covenant relationship with Adam and Eve because he created them already in communion with himself. They existed together as a family.

Noah (family)

After the flood, God made a covenant with Noah and the sign of the covenant was the rainbow in the sky. God promised to never flood the earth again. At this time, God made the covenant with Noah and all of Noah's family. In this way, the covenant was expanding from a couple (Adam and Eve) to a family (Noah and his family).

Abraham (Tribe)

God makes a Covenant with Abraham and his entire tribe, thus expanding the covenant family even further. God promises Abraham land and a multitude of descendants. The sign of this covenant was circumcision.

Moses (Nation)

When the Israelites leave Egypt, God leads them to Mt. Sinai where He presents the Commandments to Moses and makes a Covenant with the entire nation of Israel. The Covenant is sealed by Moses sprinkling the blood of a sacrificed animal on the altar and on the people. The sprinkled blood on the altar symbolizes God's commitment to the Covenant. The sacrificed animal is a sign that means "If I break this Covenant, the other person can do to me what we did to this animal". Because it would seem that you could never kill God, The Israelites are assured that God is going to keep his end of the Covenant. Later we see that the Israelites do not keep their end of the Covenant when they worship the Golden Calf.

As we fast forward to the New Testament, we see that Jesus offers us "the new and everlasting Covenant" which is sealed not in the blood of an animal but in his blood. Jesus Himself takes on the punishment for breaking the Covenant. He pays our debts and offers a new and everlasting Covenant. In the time of Moses, God promised the Israelites the land flowing with milk and honey. Jesus, however, offers the land of eternal life, which is heaven. To enter into this Covenant with Jesus we do not sprinkle his blood on us, but we do drink it in the Eucharist. "Take this all of you and drink from it, this is the Chalice of my blood, the Chalice of the New and Everlasting Covenant". There is a strong connection between what Moses did on Mt Sinai and what Jesus did on the cross and at the Last Supper. We are able to share in the new covenant by receiving Jesus in the Eucharist.

Kind David (Kingdom)

Under the rule of King David, God makes a Covenant with David and a promise that from David's line would come a ruler that would rule forever. This ruler would be Jesus Christ. The Gospel of Matthew begins with a genealogy which shows us that Mary's husband Joseph was in the line of King David. Through God's covenant with King David, the Covenant family has now grown to include the many nations in David's Kingdom.

Jesus – (Universal Covenant)

Katholicos is a Greek word for "Universal". Jesus Himself is the new and final covenant for all people. To be able to include all people, the new Covenant is not made to someone and his family members, but instead to all people through Faith in Jesus Christ.

You no longer have to be in the right earthly family. You can now enter into the eternal Covenant with God by faith.

In response to faith, we receive Baptism and are given the new family name "of the Father and of the Son, and of the Holy Spirit". We then partake of the family meal, the Eucharist, so that we might share the same blood, the Eucharist, like family members.

Credits

I took a course in college from Dr. Scott Hahn, who outlined much of the above information. Dr. Hahn has a book title *A Father Keeps His Promises,* which outlines the above in great details. Jeff Cavins also explains the above in any easy to learn format in his *The Great Adventure Bible Timeline* series.

The History of the Bible

It is important to realize that the books which make up the Bible were not officially recognized as being part of the Bible until a variety of Catholic council meetings in the 4th and 5th centuries. There are many books written about Jesus and early Christian life which are not included in the Bible. It was Catholic Bishops who helped make the distinction between which books were to be included in the Bible and which were not. And, what criteria did they use to decide which books were to be included? They were able to compare the contents of the books with the Deposit of Faith (See Apostolic Succession chapter). They were able to judge whether a book matched the sacred teachings that had been handed down to them. In other words, the assembly of the Bible is a fruit of Catholic Apostolic Tradition. The Bible, in many ways, comes from the very Catholic thing that many Protestants protest against, Catholic Apostolic Succession and the Deposit of Faith.

Questions

Name the 6 major Covenants in Scripture.

What is different about the 6th Covenant?

How does the Covenant with Moses foreshadow the Covenant with Jesus?

Are you part of a Covenant, like marriage, on earth now? Did you realize you were in a covenant?

What is the definition of a Covenant?

Do you feel like you belong to God's family?

Can you share one personal story of feeling like you belong to a family?

The Eucharist

Understanding Jesus' True Presence in the Eucharist

In #3, Covenants in Scripture, we learned that Jesus is the mediator of the new and everlasting covenant. In fact, he is the Covenant itself. In the same way that Moses sprinkled the blood of the sacrificed animal on the people to commit them to the covenant, so do we now drink the blood of the sacrificed lamb, Jesus, in order to receive the benefits of God's promises of the new covenant. But, the question often arises as to whether or not Jesus meant to offer us his true body and blood or simply asked us to symbolically remember the last supper with him.

Jesus of course says at the last supper, "Take this all of you and eat of it, this is my body", and "Take this all of you and drink of it, this is the cup of my blood, the blood of the new and everlasting covenant". While it is true that Jesus often uses stories to get his point across, it is also true that it is fairly obvious when He is doing so. For example, the Bible will say, "he told them this parable…". Or, "he spoke in parables ". When it comes to the accounts of the last supper in Matthew, Mark, and Luke, the Bible does not mention anything about a parable or a symbol. The problem with saying Jesus is speaking symbolically here is that it then calls into question a lot of the other things he said.

Fortunately, this very question was raised by some people with Jesus and their interchange is recorded in John chapter 6. To understand the Eucharist, it is important that you understand John chapter 6.

In John chapter 6, crowds of people are following Jesus and they ask him for a sign so that they may know he is sent by God. The people say to him "Our Ancestors ate manna in the dessert, as it is written: He gave them bread from heaven to eat". Jesus then tells them that it was the Father who gave them bread and that the bread given by the Father gives life to the world. The followers then asked to be given this special bread. Then Jesus said to them "I am the bread of life, whoever comes to me will never hunger..". At this point, it is possible that Jesus is speaking symbolically and if he said nothing further about it, one might believe he is speaking symbolically. Fortunately, the Jews with him said, "How can he say 'I have come down from heaven'". Jesus heard them murmuring and said, "Your ancestors ate Manna in the desert, but they died; this is the bread that came down from heaven; whoever eats of this bread will live forever; and the bread that I will give is my flesh for the life of the world."

Again, it still might seem he is speaking symbolically. Fortunately, the Jews with him believed he was speaking literally because they asked "How can this man give us flesh to eat". Now, after they asked this question, if Jesus were speaking symbolically, it would have been appropriate for him to clarify his point. This would have been his opportunity to say, "hey I'm just using metaphors...calm down".

Instead, Jesus said "Amen, Amen, I say to you, unless you [1]eat the flesh of the Son of Man and drink his blood, you do not have life within you. Whoever [2]eats my flesh and drinks my blood has eternal life, and I will raise him on the last day. For [3]my flesh is true food, and my blood is true drink. Whoever [4]eats my flesh and drinks my blood remains in me and I am in him... Just as the living Father sent me and I have life because of the Father, so also the one who feeds on me will have life because of me. This is the bread that came down from heaven. Unlike your ancestors who ate and still died, whoever eats this bread will live forever. "

At this point, I'd like to mention that Jesus answers their question about whether or not he is speaking of his flesh by saying 4 times that He is speaking about His flesh and blood.. Look back over Jesus last words and see his four statements on what he is talking about. There are little numbers in the quoted text above which count Jesus' four statements about his "true flesh and blood".

While it seems clear that Jesus was speaking literally, we are fortunate that the story drives the point home one more time.

After Jesus' above comments many of his disciples said, "This saying is hard; who can accept it?". This shows us that they took Jesus to mean these things literally as well. This also shows us that the teaching was hard for even those who heard Jesus say it. Jesus heard them state their frustration and said "The words I have spoken to you are spirit and life, but there are some of you who do not believe". John's Gospel then says, "As a result of this, many of his disciples returned to their former way of life and no longer accompanied him". Again, this would have been Jesus' moment to call the former disciples back and explain that he was speaking symbolically. Instead, he says to the twelve, "Do you also want to

32

leave". Peter answered, "Master, to whom shall we go? You have the words of eternal life".

I like to imagine that from this point forward, when those who remained with Jesus walked through town, that those who left that day would point their finger at those with Jesus and say, smirkingly, "Those are the guys that think they are going to eat their master, ha ha ha ha..They are so weird". From that day on, one of the criteria for hanging out with Jesus was believing that someday, they would "eat his flesh" and "drink his blood". Even though they believed Jesus, they must have wondered "how" it was going to happen. Because this would have become a major identifying belief of Jesus followers, I always imagine that Jesus words from this day would have been ringing in the Apostle's ears on the night of the last supper when Jesus said, "This is my body, and This is my blood". Perhaps on many occasions before when they sat down for a meal, they anticipated eating his body. But, on the night of the last supper, Jesus finally shows them how and gives them his body and blood, which as Jesus says, will be shed for you". Of course, Jesus then gives them the directive to "do this in memory of me" and so begins the tradition of celebrating the Eucharist weekly. It is also worth noting that Jesus institutes the Eucharist at the Passover meal, which was already a meal of remembrance. The meal recalls Israel's exodus from Egypt on the night that God killed the first born in Egypt. The Israelites had to kill a lamb and sprinkle its blood on their door posts so that the angel of death would not kill the first born in their homes. And so, in the same fashion, Jesus blood protects us from the eternal death that would await us, if it were not for his sacrifice and outpouring of blood. You should note that in the Passover story, the Israelites were not instructed to symbolically slaughter a lamb and pretend to spread its blood on the doorpost. They did not pretend to sprinkle animal blood on the people and the altar of God on Mt. Sinai. They really went through with the ritual and really used blood. We too really do receive pardon and safety by eating and drinking Jesus' blood.

Later after Jesus resurrection, when Jesus appears to a couple disciples on the Road to Emmaus, he talks to them at great length but they don't recognize him as Jesus. When he comes into their home and "breaks bread" with them, it says they "recognized him the breaking of the bread" and then he vanished from their presence. Perhaps at the moment they realized he was present in the breaking of the bread. He left in his bodily form because they now grasped how he could "remain with you always".

In St Paul's letters, he encourages his readers to not approach the body and blood of Christ unworthily because 'if you do so, you will condemn yourself'. This is very strong language if the Eucharist is only a symbol. It seems Paul took the Eucharist literally as well.

In fact, most Christians took the Eucharist literally for 1,500 years. It was not until the Reformation that the true presence in the Eucharist was called into question. Again, if the Christian faith had at this point been wrong for 1,500 years, how can anyone know for sure which points were right or wrong over the period of those 1,500 years? The problem discussed earlier of having a religion without Apostolic Succession comes into play here.

Personally, with all of the above evidence, I'm not sure why you wouldn't want to believe in the Eucharist. To me, it is another way that Jesus has created to be with us. He did not go to heaven and leave us here to "figure things out" on our own. He has remained with us in the breaking of the bread. I personally have found great comfort and a powerful presence in the Eucharist. Many times when praying in a chapel with the Eucharist, I have a sense that some "one" is in the room with me. And this person has a remarkable power to "make my heart burn within". In addition, it seems hard for me to believe that the grace which seems to rush through my mind after receiving the Eucharist is only psychological. I realize Jesus leaves room for doubt for those who don't believe. But, based on my experiences, I believe. In fact, it is a bit more than believing- Jesus presence in the Eucharist has become a normal part of my life. He is another person with whom I interact. How do I know for sure that my other friends exist? How do I know that my parents exist? Maybe they are just part of my imagination? Sometimes we have confidence in people because well, we "know" them. I am thankful to "know" Jesus, especially in the Eucharist. I am happy to have received such an undeserved grace, and I believe this grace is for all of us.

Catholics believe that at each Catholic Mass, the bread and the wine become the body and blood of Christ. We believe that the nature of bread and wine become the nature of Jesus Christ. We believe, by a miracle, that the nature changes while the appearance of bread and wine remains. You could say that the miracle is the changing of the nature or you could say that the miracle is the keeping of the appearance of the bread and the wine. Either way, Jesus miraculously becomes present. The fancy word used for this is "Transubstantiation", which means the substance changes. While this concept may be hard to grasp, it shouldn't be too difficult for someone of a Christian faith to grasp. After all, Christians believe that an ordinary man was also God. To a non-Christian, without the gift of faith, Jesus being God is also a ridiculous proposition. Without the gift of faith, bread and wine becoming Jesus is also a crazy proposition. However, in the realm of Christianity, it isn't such an unlikely situation. Once you have admitted God became man, was crucified, died, and rose from the dead, is there really much room to doubt the possibilities of him doing anything else he wants to do? Like, St Peter, if you hang out with Jesus long enough, you would likely also say, "Lord, to whom else would we go. You have the words of everlasting life".

Questions

Can you summarize John Chapter 6? If so, try to do so no in your group?

Have you been in conversations before with other people about the True Presence if Jesus in the Eucharist?

Would information like this help you in those conversations?

What struck you most from reading this section?

Do you think this information will affect your prayer time or prayer during Mass?

Can you share a personal experiences about experiencing Jesus' presence in the Eucharist?

The Five Precepts of the Church

Minimum Requirements for Being Catholic

The 5 precepts are a fantastic thing to know about Catholicism. Many people think the list of what they have to do be Catholic is very long and exhaustive. They will likely be surprised to see how short the list is. On the other hand, there are some items on this list that some people think are optional, when in fact they are required.

I hope this list frees you from unnecessary burdens and at the same time helps you keep your Baptismal Commitments to the Church.

The Precepts of the Church

1. Attend Mass on Sundays and holy days of obligation and rest from servile labor
   Go to Mass on Sundays and Holy Days of Obligation

2. Confess your sins at least once a year.
   Go to Confession at least once per year.

3. Receive the sacrament of the Eucharist at least during the Easter season

4. Observe the days of fasting and abstinence established by the Church
   *Ash Wed and Good Friday Fasting and Abstain from meat, Fridays in Lent abstain from meat, do some kind of penance every day in Lent except Sundays, Do some kind of penance every Friday outside of Lent. *Note when Solemnities fall on days of penance, you don't have to do penance. Solemnities are like Sundays!*

5. Help to provide for the needs of the Church according to your ability
   Donate to the Church and those in need

These 5 precepts presume you are following the 10 Commandments as well.

Questions

What are the five precepts of the Church?

Which precepts were you surprised to see on this list?

Where there any items you thought should be on the list but are surprised to find are not?

Which will be the hardest for you to keep?

Share your personal experience with each of the precepts of the Church.

The 7 Sacraments

Essential Signs, Words, and Graces

Every Sacrament has specific elements which must be present for the sacrament to take place. For example with Baptism, water must be poured over the head three times (or the person dunked in water 3x) along with the words of "I baptize you in the name of the Father and of the Son and of the Holy Spirit". As long as the water is used 3x and the right word are said, a person is validly Baptized. In its strictest essence, Baptism can be performed by a non-Baptized person on another non-Baptized person. So, you could be traveling with a non-baptized friend and enter into a car accident. Lying in the ruble of the crash and fearing death, you could ask your non-Christian friend to Baptize you with the Dasani bottled water in the cup holder. If your friend used the right words and put the water on your head three times, you would in fact receive the graces of Baptism.

In non-emergency circumstances however, the Church asks that you go through a formation process and receive Baptism in a

Church by a priest or a deacon. Babies are also baptized in a Church by a priest or deacon.

In normal circumstances, we tend to add other elements to the rite of Baptism that while symbolically helpful, do not make up the essence of Baptism. For example, it is customary to hand the Godparents of the newly Baptized adult a candle that has been lit from the Easter Candle. This is nicely symbolic but is not an essential part of Baptism. We also add many prayers before the essential rite, that again while helpful, are not essential to the sacrament. I think it is important to know the essential elements so that you a) know when to really pay attention and b) focus with the highest priority on the essential elements and avoid giving undue attention to the decorative elements. I think of all the other things surrounding a sacrament as "decorative rites" because they decorate or dress up the "essential rite". And, this is okay and good. We dress up our bodies with nice clothes, nice hair, and accessories for big events. It makes sense to dress up Sacraments. However, it is just very healthy to learn what the essential rite is and what it is not. Imagine picking your date up for Prom and thinking you are actually dating her dress or her hair. This sounds ridiculous but over thousands of years, without proper explanation, we can start to emphasize the wrong elements of the Sacraments. It would be no surprise that you might leave your prom dates during the night because you felt that her hair just didn't talk back to you enough. Likewise, if people don't understand the essential components of the sacraments and Catholicism, it might not be surprising that they are leaving the Church.

Understanding Sacraments

Sacraments are guaranteed encounters with God's grace. You might ask "why even have sacraments?" There is some truth to your inquiry because we do believe that God is bigger than His sacraments. We don't think God is confined to or limited to his sacraments. In other words, he can, if he wants, dispense the grace of any sacrament to you without you receiving the sacrament. However, we don't have as much certainty when we go that route. We have certainty about the graces received from the Sacraments because they were instituted by Christ for the purpose of providing their respective graces. Of course God can forgive your sins without a priest....but he has guaranteed to forgive and absolve your sins via a priest.

I like to bet on sure things, which is why I love sacraments. Imagine a father who tells his daughters that he will pass out a $20 allowance every Friday at 5pm in the kitchen of the house. Week after week the girls collect their allowance. But, one week, the daughters are in their bedroom at 4:45pm and one of the girls is sleeping. The awake one says to the asleep one, "wake up, dad is going to give out our allowance in 15 minutes". The asleep one, awakes a little bit to say "Ohh, no worries, I'll ask dad for it some other time". Now, the sleeping daughter may be right. She might be able to ask dad for it another time. On the other hand, dad, the one she plans to ask, did set out some pretty clear guidelines about when and how he would give out the allowance. As I mentioned, I like a sure thing, so I would be heading down to the kitchen a bit before 5:00pm to make sure I'm there for the promised allowance.

You can insert any sacrament in the place of the allowance. Sure, God is bigger than his sacraments and he doesn't "need" them, but perhaps we do. In the case of Baptism, Jesus did give clear directives to go out into all the world and Baptize in the name of the Father and of the son and of the Holy Spirit. Baptism is not an optional sacrament. And, because the Church requires us to receive the Eucharist and Confession once per year, they are not optional either. Confirmation completes Baptismal grace, so it is a great idea to pick that one up to.

The next pages show a table for every sacrament listing its essential elements as well as its effect or grace. The matter/sign row shows what physical elements must be present for the sacrament to work. The Words row shows what must be said out loud. The Minister row lists the actual people required for the sacrament to work. We noted that Baptism just needs a living person. On the other hand, Holy Orders requires a Bishop and the Eucharist requires a priest or Bishop. The final row called Graces lists the many benefits of receiving the particular sacrament.

Baptism

Sacrament	Baptism
Matter/Sign	Water poured on head 3x or immersion in water 3x
Words	"I Baptize you in the name of the Father and of the Son and of the Holy Spirit"
Minister	Essentially: any person Normative: Priest or Deacon
Graces	forgiveness of sin receive Holy Spirit new creature enter Church (body of Christ) indelible spiritual mark unity with other Christians

We already discussed most of Baptism. I encourage you to read through the cells on the above table. Baptism is the first sacrament that we receive and it must be received before any other sacrament. Baptism forgives original sin, all sin, and gives us the Holy Spirit.

Confirmation

Sacrament	Confirmation
Matter/Sign	Laying on of hands and anointing with oil
Words	Be Sealed with the gift of the Holy Spirit
Minister	Priest or Bishop (in eastern rites the priest is normative)
Graces	unites more firmly with Christ increases gifts of Holy Spirit in us more perfect bond with Church grace to boldly witness to Christ completes Baptismal grace indelible spiritual mark

The matter or sign of Confirmation is the laying on of hands and anointing with oil. Essentially a priest is required but in the Latin Catholic Rites, a Bishop normally performs Confirmations. In the Eastern Catholic Rites, a priest almost always administers Confirmation at the same time as Baptism. Even infants receive Confirmation in the Eastern Catholic Churches. Eastern Catholic Churches or Rites are still 100% Catholic. However, their liturgies would look a lot like Eastern Orthodox celebrations. Especially in the early Church before Christian was legal and communication was easy, the successors of the Apostles developed different styles for the way they celebrated the Sacraments. They kept the sacraments themselves in tact they just added different decorative elements and styles. After Christianity became legal in the Roman Empire and as communication become easier, it was easier to standardize the celebration of the liturgy. However, the Eastern rites were allowed to keep their traditions. Because members of the Western or Roman rite explored the Americas, it becamse the case that most of the Americas are Roman rite, hence the phrase "Roman Catholic". However, there are Byzantine Catholics, Maronite Catholics,

Melkite Catholics etc. All of them are Catholic. There is only one "western" rite, which is the Roman rite and many Eastern rites.

Confirmation has connections to Baptism because it completes Baptismal grace and and is a sacrament of initiation. Confirmation is also connected to the Bishop because in the early Church Apostles were able to perform many Confirmations. However, as the Church grew, it became impossible for Apostles and their successors to be at every Confirmation. In the West, this problem was solved by moving Confirmation to an older age so that many people of the same age could be gathered together at once to receive Confirmation from the Bishop. In the Eastern Churches, they wanted to emphasize Confirmation connection to Baptism, so priests began Confirming babies just after Baptizing them. To keep some connection with the Bishop, these priests use oil blessed by the local Bishop. Easter rite Churches also give the Eucharist to babies.

Confirmation is a very very powerful sacrament that has its historical roots in Pentecost. While already members of Jesus fold, the Apostles did not fully grasp or begin their Apostolic Ministry until the were immersed in or anointed by the Holy Spirit at Pentecost. In seeing this experience, many jews present at Pentecost desired to be Baptized. In the same way, Confirmation allows to receive and participate in the graces of Pentecost so that we can understand our own Baptism and more powerfully and effectively preach and minister God's presence to others. Our ministry in the power of the Holy Spirit leads others to Baptism. Like Holy Orders is a sacrament that is given to a man for the Church, so is Confirmation a sacrament given to individuals "for the Church". Even if we don't recall much from the day of our Confirmation, we received a lot of powerful grace that has been stored inside of us. Don't be afraid to ask God to let you know on a personal level what you were actual given in your Confirmation.

Eucharist

Sacrament	Eucharist
Matter/Sign	Bread and Wine
Words	Take this, all of you, and eat of it: for this is my body which will be given up for you. Take this, all of you, and drink from it: for this is the chalice of my blood, the blood of the new and eternal covenant, which will be poured out for you and for many for the forgiveness of sins . Do this in memory of me.
Minister	Priest or Bishop
Graces	union with Christ separates us from sin – prevents mortal sin unity with mystical body of Christ, the Church commits us to the poor unity with other Christians

We really covered this Sacrament in the chapter on the Eucharist. A few neat notes about this Sacrament is that it does forgive venial sin and helps prevent mortal sin. A priest or a Bishop must say the words of consecration over bread and wine. There are some rules that govern the make-up of the bread and wine but for the most part it should be unleavened bread and wine of a certain alcoholic content without preservatives. In other words, you cannot convert cookies and milk to the body and blood of Jesus.

Marriage

Sacrament	Marriage
Matter/Sign	consummation / life together
Words	Wedding Vows and a few key questions before the vows. 1) Oneness – sex and spiritual union 2) Fruitfulness –sexual acts are open to life 3) Faithfulness – only with each other 4) Permanence – until death
Minister	**Latin Rite:** Man and Woman exclusively **Eastern Rites:** Man, Woman, and Priest as witness
Graces	Receive Christ via Spouse (receptive emphasis) Grace to perfect love and holiness Children Image Trinity to the World

There is an upcoming chapter on Marriage so I encourage you to read that chapter for a fuller understanding of marriage. But, a few quick points from the chart: Marriage is between a baptized man and a baptized woman and they confer the sacrament on each other. In the Eastern rite a priest is part of the essential rite. Any two baptized people can receive this Sacrament. Both do not have to be Catholic but both must be baptized. Marriage between a Catholic and non-baptized person can still be a life-long covenantal commitment, but it can't be a sacrament.

Holy Orders

Sacrament	Marriage
Matter/Sign	laying on of hands
Words	Specific prayer of ordination and outpouring of the Holy Spirit for the gifts proper to the ministry to which the candidate is being ordained: deacon, priest or bishop
Minister	Bishop
Graces	Indelible spiritual character Grace of the Holy Spirit for each particular role: Bishop, Priest, Deacon

Holy Orders is conferred by the laying on of hands of a Bishop to baptized man. Certain prayers must be said. There are three versions or steps of Holy Orders: Deacon, Priest, and Bishop. A Bishop has the fullness of Holy Orders and the other Orders in some way are a participation in the Vocation of the Bishopric. Priests serve Bishops and Deacons serve priests. Holy Orders provides an indelible spiritual mark on the man's soul such that it can never be removed. Even if one is dismissed of his commitments to the priesthood, he will always be sacramentally speaking, a priest, deacon, or Bishop. Holy Orders is a very important Sacrament because it helps preserve the Church and the sacraments.

It is also helpful to the laity to understand the essence of Holy Orders so as not to place undue burdens and expectations on priests and Bishops. As you look over the Chart or Table of Sacraments above, you'll see that some sacraments require a priest. In this way, one of the primary functions of a priest is to provide these sacraments. We should be thankful that some men have been called and responded to the call to be priests to offer us these sacraments, especially the Eucharist and Confession. Many other roles that priests tend to do are not essential to Holy Orders. Managing a large parish is not essential to the sacrament of Holy Orders. Being good at counseling or teaching is also not essential to Holy Orders. We should acknowledge that not all men are going to be great at all elements of church ministry. Priests too can be relieved of unnecessary burdens by focusing on their sacramental duties and serving within their areas of giftedness. Areas outside their giftedness can be left to other priests or laity more equipped to serve in those areas. We don't have to expect priests to do it all and they don't need to do it all. Laity should step up to serve where they are gifted and where their parish is in need. On the other extreme, laity should not make attempts to perform sacraments or step over the line of their area of service. All of this can be confusing to us because we see some Protestant Minsters excelling in certain areas and we start to judge our priests by those standards.

Reconciliation / Confession

Sacrament	Confession
Matter/Sign	All by the Penitent 1. Contrition 2. Confession 3. Penance
Words	"I absolve you from your sins"
Minister	Priest or Bishop
Graces	Absolution of sins Strength to not sin again Reconciliation with the Church

This is a wonderful sacrament. At its roots, it is a sacrament that solves the problem of serious sin after Baptism. It is possible to sin so badly and on purpose that you break your relationship with God and the Church. These are called mortal sins and they require knowledge of their severity as well as willingness to do them anyway. However, it is possibly to break our relationship with the family of God and because Baptism is a one-time Sacrament, we need a way for people who repent of such sins to be sacramentally forgiven and reconciled to God and the Church. This is the primary role of Confession or Reconciliation. However, this sacrament is not only for such sins and can be very helpful for spiritual growth and absolution of venial sins. The Sacrament does contain within it the power to help you to never sin again, especially in the areas confessed. It is not just a sacrament of forgiveness for the past but a grace of power for the future. The precepts of the Church call us to receive this sacrament at least once per year.

A priest must give the sacrament and a baptized person who is sorry for their sins must confess their sins and do the given penance. Sorrow or Contrition can be of two kinds: perfect or imperfect. Imperfect contrition is based on your fear of the punishment of sin. Perfect contrition is rooted in your desire to do good and your sorrow for offending God. Either way, you have contrition and qualify to receive this sacrament. The sins must be said out loud to a priest in person. The priest will say the words of absolution and provide a penance, which is usually a prayer or action to help show our converted heart. Completing the penance by the penitent is part of the essential rite of the sacrament. You must do the penance to finish the sacrament.

Confession is a powerful sacrament and one that is often avoided due to the humbling action of confessing sins to another person. However, the sacrament is real and does have power. At times, I've avoided near occasions of sin not even so much out of fear of God but out of fear of having to say the sin to a priest. This would be a worldly benefit but a benefit nonetheless. There is something therapeutic and healing by forcing yourself to verbalize your repentance. One bit of encouraging advice would be to focus on your "conversion" or new heart and not as much on the horrible wretchedness of your sins. Be sorry for your sins and seek a clean slate. After all, your Father has promised to absolve your sins when you receive this sacrament. The more you picture Jesus as the one you confess to, the easier it will likely be make your confession. Then, on a human level, priests assure me that it is impossible to remember yours sins as distinct from the hundreds or thousands of confessions they hear each year. On that note, you really probably can't say something they haven't heard before. Further, while your confession should be somewhat specific, it does not need to be graphic. The priest will get the picture easily enough.

This sacrament is also not about you knowing how you will be able to avoid sin again. You don't have to be perfect to repent. Repenting is just admitting you've been on the wrong side of the fence, that you've rationalized God's law, that you told yourself something was okay when you knew deep down it was not.

Repenting is admitting you were wrong and seeking God's pardon and help to never sin again.

Anointing of the Sick

Sacrament	Anointing of the Sick
Matter/Sign	laying on of hands
Words	Specific prayer of Anointing
Minister	Bishop or Priest
Graces	Strength, healing, forgiveness of sin

In the Anointing of the Sick, a priest or Bishop lays hands on the sick person and anoints them with oil, and a special prayer is prayed. The primary aim of this sacrament is for physical healing. Many times we associate this sacrament with "last rites" or something nice we do before someone dies. It surely does provide strength and healing and forgiveness in those situations. However, at its root, Anointing of the Sick seeks to provide healing just as Jesus healed the sick. We might all benefit from brining more expectant faith to this sacrament.

Questions

Can you list the 7 sacraments?

Every sacrament has four components...what are those four components?

What is the sign for the Sacrament of Holy Orders?

What are the words for the Sacrament of Reconciliation?

Which sacrament did you know the least about before reading this chapter? What did you learn?

Can you share a personal experience about receiving one of the sacraments?

The 10 Commandments

and Evaluating the Morality of an Act

An act is considered moral if both its means and end are good. The means is "how" the act is done and the end is the actual goal or reason for doing the act. A classic example is stealing to give to the poor. Giving to the poor is an end goal that is good. But, stealing as a means is not good. You can never do something that is morally wrong regardless of the end goal. Both the means and the end must be good. You also should not do good things with a bad end goal in mind. This principle of means and ends is used frequently in sexual and medical moral decisions. Many times it looks like something immoral could be done because of the good intention or end goal. However, in Catholic morality, ends do not justify the means. One example is abortion. You cannot end the baby's life on purpose to save the mother's life. Causing on purpose one death violates a moral law even if the end goal is saving another life. Following this principle can call for some very heroic decisions and behavior. In following this principle we find that life is not necessarily fair and that suffering is often encountered. Instead of dismissing our religion on these points, we might find some comfort in seeing that these tough moments remind us that life on earth is not the final life. Life on earth is not perfect because of sin, including our sin. We don't have a "right" or really much of any ability to make life on earth perfect. We do our best and pray for "on earth as it is in heaven" but we can be reminded that in heaven, ends do not justify immoral means either. There is suffering and we will die. It is nice to know however that we can rise above those two evils and do the right thing. Doing the right thing is much more eternal and life giving than the limited reward offered by sin.

Another few things to consider when evaluating a moral act are the three elements of object, intention, circumstance. The object is the actual act itself. It is a lot like the "means" in the above example. If the object is bad, then the action can be objectively called "immoral". However, the intention and circumstance determine to what degree the guilty party is in fact guilty. Because we can't ever know fully one's intentions and because the circumstances are often quite complex, it is not possible for us to "judge" people's souls. We cannot know all the elements involved as God can. However, that does not mean we cannot identify immoral "objects" or actions as immoral. We can say that adultery is wrong and that Joe should not have done it. But, we can't in any way judge or claim to judge Joe's soul and the degree of sinfulness in the matter.

Sometimes we judge too much and interfere with people's lives too much. On the other extreme, sometimes we take the phrase "don't judge" and stop identifying what is wrong and evil. We can't let the devil slip into the garden unnoticed. We might not know the details of the soul of the person who let him in, but once he is in, we can sure sound the alarm and call evil, "evil".

The 10 Commandments

1. **You Shall Worship the Lord Your God and Him Alone Shall You Serve**

   We keep the first commandment by keeping God as the #1 thing in our lives. While we might not be tempted to carve statue idols and worship them, we are tempted to put other things before God. It is usually fairly simple to evaluate your obedience to this commandment. Simply ask yourself, "What is the #1 most important thing in my life?" What do I think about most of the time? While it is true that your life might require a lot of work and a lot of other tasks, you can usually always tell deep down inside whether God is #1 or #2 or #3. A lot of times, when we ask ourselves, we find that we do want God to be #1 but our thoughts and time have not been spent accordingly. In these cases, we can work to move God to the #1 spot by scheduling prayer and acts of service into our daily and weekly plans. We can make appointments with God (prayer time) just as we would make any other appointment. You might have an appointment with a professor at 2pm on Monday. Despite all you have going on, you'll likely make that appointment. Why will you make it? Because deep down your academic success is of very high priority to you. The same can be   true   with   God.

2. **You Shall Not Take the Name of the Lord Your God in vain**

   Here we learn that God's name is in fact holy. The name itself has power and refers to Him, the Holy God. To use his name is to invoke Him, to call on Him, to ask for his aid. As such, we should reserve His name for its proper use. We should not take his name in vain, which would mean swearing an oath by His name or using His name as an expression of frustration or in cursing. You probably instinctively would not use your mother's name to curse or to try and prove to someone that you are telling the truth. In the same way, we should respect God's name.

On the positive side, this commandment reminds us that God's name is holy and does have power. We can call on Him to aid us. He has revealed Himself fully to us in the person and in the name of Jesus. Calling on Jesus has power and can be of great help.

3. **Remember the Sabbath day, to keep it holy. Six days you shall labor, and do all your work; but the seventh day is a Sabbath to the Lord your God; in it you shall not do any work.**

Our primary duty on the Sabbath (Sunday) is to attend Sunday Mass or the Vigil Mass on Saturday night. We should also refrain from servile labor that is so difficult that it takes us away from the spirit of the Lord 's Day. As a student, you can read and study on the Sabbath. However, if your tasks were so challenging that they ruined your mood and removed your mind from the restful and holy disposition of Sunday, then perhaps you should try to refrain from those tasks. Exercising is okay on the Sabbath and doing works of service for others is a great idea on the Sabbath. If your employment is light work and the shifts are short, you can also work on the Sabbath. An example given by Pope John Paul II was of someone who worked a four hour shift in a movie theater. Running the movie real is not very grueling work, the hours are not long, and the work provides relaxation for those watching the movie. People's dispositions are different, so you'll have to figure out for you, what constitutes a servile labor that distracts from the Lord's Day.

In most cases, you should be able to plan to attend Sunday Mass. You know that it is coming every week for the rest of your life. You can plan trips and vacations accordingly.

4. **Honor your father and your mother, that your days may be long in the land which the Lord your God gives you.**

   This commandment has a promise attached to it, so it might really be worth obeying. To honor your parents does not mean they get to your control lives for the rest of your lives. When you are very young however, it does mean they pretty much can control your lives. As you get older, the balance between who is calling the shots shifts. College is a particularly difficult time because in many ways you are old enough to make your own life decisions. On the other hand, you haven't made a lot of life decisions yet and your parents are probably still providing for you financially and in many other ways. Before you decide you are fully in charge, it might be worth asking yourself whether you really could provide for yourself and truly be in charge. The change in authority from parents to children is delicate and both should be sensitive to the time of transfer. It doesn't magically happen at a certain age unfortunately.

   In extreme cases, parents can be doing something very wrong or immoral. For example in the case of child abuse, no child has a moral obligation to stay with their parents and endure the abuse. In fact, they should seek safety and protection. On the other hand, parents should not be afraid to exercise their authority.

   Outside of rules and conduct, children should foster a spirit of "honor' for their parents during their entire lives. Parents help mirror our relationship with God and they do many god-like things. For this, children do owe their parents honor. My advice to children would be to error on the side of honor and obedience. God has promised "that your days would be long in the land which the Lord your God gives you". Even if you think your parents are a bit silly, it can't hurt to have more of God's grace on your side.

5. **You shall not kill.**

Here of course murder is outlawed. But, there are many ways that we can attack or kill the spirit of another. Doing any intentional harm to another violates this commandment. Doing harm to yourself also violates this commandment. Abusing alcohol or drugs, over eating, failing to exercise, and other bad habits also fall under this commandment because you are hurting yourself.

On the other hand, some cases might lead to the ending of life that do not violate this law. Stated another way, this law reads, "You shall not take innocent life". Defending your own life in such a way that the attacker's life ends, would not be a violation of this commandment. Your intention was to protect your life and the sad consequence was ending the life of the person trying to hurt of kill you.

It may also be worth noting that this law makes a distinction between abortion and the death penalty. Assuming the death penalty is enacted on a truly guilty party, the ending of the criminal's life does not violate this commandment. However, as Pope John Paul II pointed out, with modern incarceration facilities, it is possible to protect society from dangerous criminals and allow the criminal to live out his or her life naturally. While the death penalty for guilty parties does not violate the law of justice, it does not live up to the call for mercy. In a small Western town in the 1800s, it probably made logical sense to end the life of a serial killer. There was perhaps no way to contain the serial killer and prevent further harm to the citizens of the town. The death penalty may have been just to the killer and charitable to the citizens. But, with modern incarceration facilities, a Christian society can move past justice and extend mercy to the criminal.

However, under no circumstances would abortion not violate this commandment. The unborn child is never guilty and thus ending her life would never constitute a just death.

6. You Shall Not commit adultery
This commandment covers actual adultery as well as all violations against chastity. Much more on this topic is covered in the marriage section.

7. You Shall Not Steal
Private property is to be respected, which includes physical goods and intellectual content. However a case can be made on a global decade long scale regarding the ownership of land. On the one hand, land ownership is important for progress, safety, and privacy. On the other, it is possible for governments and groups to accumulate an innapropriate amount of land, especially when that land ownership is denying other nearby humans their normal rights to life. The line here on what

constitutes private property and what constitutes a call for massive land to be divided can be very tricky. It is simply worth noting that while private property is important and to be respected, the right to human ownership of things is not absolute in all cases.

8. **You shall not bear false witness against your neighbor.**
   This commandment covers telling the truth and not lying. Lying is withholding the truth from anyone who deserves to know it. Therefore, circumstances may arise where you do not reveal the truth to someone because the person does not have a right to know. For example, a total stranger asks you for the dates of your vacation and your home address. It would be in your interest to not reveal this information and you would not be "lying" because the asker has no right to the information. The classic example imagines a person being asked during World War II in Germany if he were hiding Jews in his home. In order to further protect the lives of those in hiding, it would not be lying to answer "no" even if one were hiding a Jewish family in the home. On the other hand, when the parents ask a child where he is going, the parents have a right to know and withholding the information or giving false information is a lie.

9 + 10. You shall not covet your neighbor's house; you shall not covet your neighbor's wife, or his manservant, or his maidservant, or his ox, or his ass, or anything that is your neighbor's.

By avoiding the desires for another's spouse or goods to arise up within us, we are better able to avoid some of the commandments listed above. In these commandments we are given an insight into

Jesus comments that "Everyone who looks at a woman lustfully has already committed adultery with her in his heart". These two commandments show us that we are not only responsible for our actions but for the degree to which we let feeling and thoughts carry on inside of us. Of course to a certain degree we cannot escape certain thoughts and desires. But, we do have some control over how much we foster these feelings. The part of the act of contrition prayer which says, "and to avoid the near occasion of sin" applies here. Knowing that we can become enslaved to our passions, we should not then put ourselves in situations or prolong situations that ignite disordered passions.

In the lust for another's position or goods, we might also find a lack of hope and charity towards ourselves. For some reason we think another person is better or more deserving because of his/her surroundings. Perhaps we can allow God to love us more and perhaps we can believe and work more ourselves towards building for ourselves the surroundings we desire, assuming those surroundings are good and pure. Sometimes we might covet another's goods as a way of failing to admit that our lack of good's is not due to luck or chance but to our bad habits or poor financial management. Taking care of our own surroundings is a great way to prevent the temptation of coveting another's. By working hard ourselves, we can also gain a respect and appreciation for the hard work of our neighbor and be happy for his or her accomplishments and possessions.

Questions

Which commandment do you think is the hardest to follow?

Did you learn anything new about one of the commandments today?

Can you share a story in which you made the right choice to follow a commandment?

Catholic Social Teaching

In the past couple centuries, much has been written by Popes regarding the ordering and structuring of society. The Catholic Church has not put together an official list of Catholic Social Teaching themes; however there are a few key themes to point out. These teaching are reflections and logical conclusions drawn from the 10 Commandments and the life and teachings of Jesus.

Human Life

We believe that human life is made in the image and likeness of God by God, and therefore it must be protected. The intentional taking of human life can never be deemed morally acceptable, even if it supposedly helps the "common good". The only exception would be in cases of self-defense. But, in these cases, the direct protection of a human life is the goal, which has an unfortunate consequence, the ending another human life. Human life is sacred from conception, through all of life, and until death.

Family and Community

God Himself is familial – Father, Son, and Holy Spirit. As such, so are His people. The immediate human family and marriage are sacred and the foundation of human relationships and unity.

Responsibility

We have a responsibility to integrate all humans into a familial and communal environment and see to it that they have the required resources to live a healthy and communal life. The poor, because of their immediate lack and need, receive preferential treatment in our steps to bring about the kingdom "on earth as it is in heaven". Jesus also speaks very severely regarding his evaluation of our treatment of those in need. Employers and governments and those with authority also have a responsibility to prevent abuse of employers and citizens. We also have a responsibility to care for and respect the earth and God's creation.

Subsidiarity

In our quest for experiencing the kingdom of heaven on earth, we are called to honor the fundamental structures and communities God established. A higher form of government or organization should not prevent a lower or smaller community, most notably the family, from having the first opportunity to fulfill social responsibilities. In other words, a higher form of government should not do what a lower form of government or a family should do, unless absolutely necessary.

Service

The final section in this book discusses our unique callings and giftedness for serving the world and the Church with power and anointing of God's love.

Questions

Describe one of the themes of Catholic Social Teaching.

What did you learn that you did not know about Catholic Social Teaching?

The Four Elements of Marriage

and the Main Principle of Sexual Morality

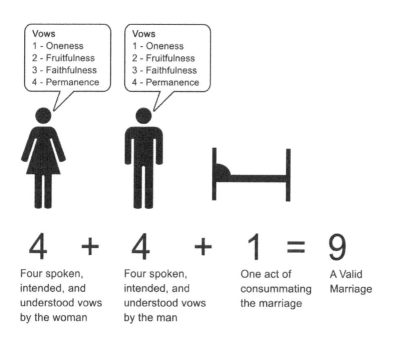

Vows
1 - Oneness
2 - Fruitfulness
3 - Faithfulness
4 - Permanence

Vows
1 - Oneness
2 - Fruitfulness
3 - Faithfulness
4 - Permanence

4 + 4 + 1 = 9

| Four spoken, intended, and understood vows by the woman | Four spoken, intended, and understood vows by the man | One act of consummating the marriage | A Valid Marriage |

A little bit of simple math can help us understand the Catholic notion of Marriage very well. In the marriage ceremony, the man and the woman must exchange vows. They are also asked a few questions before the vows which are important as well. The questions and the vows cover 4 major points. Each spouse must say and intend these four major points. The man's four and the woman's four are the two fours in the above equation. The 1 is their act of consummating the marriage (making love the first time). In order for the sacrament and the marriage to officially take place, the four vows much be exchanged, understood, and intended by each spouse and they must together consummate the marriage.

Exchanging the vows but never consummating the marriage results in an official marriage. Or, not saying, not understanding, or not intending any one of the vows also invalidates the marriage.

Annulments

Annulments are not Catholic divorces but rather decisions or pronouncements that a total of 9 was never reached on the wedding day. In the case of annulments, the big question is whether or not 9 was reached on the wedding day. Annulments do not consider how faithful the spouses were to the vows after the wedding day. Annulments are concerned with the wedding day only. The sobriety of the spouses on the wedding day can also drastically affect their willing participation in the wedding and can constitute grounds for an annulment. If the man and woman willing participate but the man does not want to have children at all, then he is withholding one of the vows and the total would only reach 8 (4+3+1) and thus there would be grounds for annulment. Because this is all a very big deal, those preparing couples for marriage should take very special care to mention and explain the 4 major vows and the requirement of consummation. The couple should be fully aware of the severity of the covenant and exactly what it entails.

The 4 Vows

While covered via the pre-vow questions and the vows themselves, the four major components that must be understood, said, and intended are:

1. **Oneness** – sexual unity and spiritual unity
2. **Fruitfulness** – every sexual act is open to life and the marriage itself is open to God's grace
3. **Faithfulness** – the above oneness and fruitfulness is to be shared exclusively between these two people (no adultery) and each spouse is to keep the other as his her #2 priority with God being the only #1.
4. **Permanence** – The commitment to be one, fruitful, and faithful lasts until one of the partners dies. A valid marriage only ends at death.

Oneness

As mentioned in the 4+4+1, the 1 stands for consummating the marriage. A valid marriage includes making love. In addition to physical unity however, Oneness involves a call to spiritual unity.

Fruitfulness

Every sexual act needs to be open to life. The reason this is the case is because sex is the sign/matter of the Sacrament. In the Sacraments section we discussed the sign, words, and minister of every sacrament. We discussed that soft drinks cannot be used in the place of the wine for the Eucharist. In Marriage, sex must be open to life because it is the sign of the words. The words include an openness to life. The sexual act "says" the same thing as the vows so it must say all of the vows every time. To make love without an openness to life would be to say something different with the body than what the couple swore they would say on their wedding day. The Church teaching on contraception is not an invasive limiting rule on marriage but a reminder of what the couple themselves made an oath to do and be on their wedding day.

However, there may be cases in which the couple does not want to conceive a child. In these cases, the couple can abstain from making love during the fertile time periods of the woman's cycle. With the use of in home testing machines as well as temperature and other bodily sign indicators, one can fairly accurately determine the window of fertility. In extreme cases where pregnancy should be avoided, the couple only needs to add more days of abstinence to both sides of the fertile window to further assure they will not conceive.

One might suggest that this abstinence method is just another form of contraception. Technically speaking it is not contraception because there is no barrier or chemical that is working "contra" or against conception. In this way the couple is keeping the sexual act congruent with the wedding vows. I like to call it the 100% principle. Each spouse must give 100% of each other in the marital act because the wedding vows call for a lifelong 100% gift of self. Contraception violates the 100% principle because the fertile part of one or both of the spouses is intentionally withheld. "I love all of you, except your fertile part". When the couple makes love in non-fertile times on purpose they do not in that particular act, violate the 100% principle because at that moment, the wife is still giving 100%. Nature itself has removed the fertile part and the wife is not intentionally holding that back. In addition, because contraception is not used, the couple still is "open to life" because it is always possible that something abnormal happens in the woman's cycle and a pregnancy could occur.

However, that being said, you may recall or want to review the section on the morality of an act. In that section, we mentioned that

72

an act must be evaluated on both its means and ends. Not conceiving children for a grave reason is a legitimate "end" or goal. In these cases, abstinence during non-fertile times is a legitimate "means" of not conceiving. In these cases, both the end and means qualify as good. It would be possible to have an illegitimate end, the selfish desire to not having children for no serious reason and then use a legitimate means of not conceiving such as times sexual encounters. In this case, the end is bad but the means is good. As a whole, the act cannot be called good. On the reverse, a very grave and legitimate reason to not conceive does not make contraception a good means. You really have to understand means and ends as two separate things in which both must be good. See the below chart:

Means		Ends		Overall Morality of the Act
Abstain during fertile periods	✔	Avoid conception for serious Reason	✔	✔
Abstain during fertile periods	✔	Avoid conception for selfish reason	✘	✘
Contraception	✘	Avoid conception for serious Reason	✔	✘
Contraception	✘	Avoid conception for selfish reason	✘	✘

You need two Green Checkmarks for the act as a whole to be considered morally good. The critique that abstinence methods could be used immorally is a valid critique if and when the "ends" receives a red x. However, those who make that critique are often defending contraception, which always receives a red check.

Faithfulness

The third element of Marriage is Faithfulness. Faithfulness defines the "who" of the oneness and fruitfulness. "I will be united to and open to life with you and only you". Strictly speaking, faithfulness refers to sexual union with your spouse only. However, on the spiritual realm, the marriage covenant calls the couple to be faithful to each other in spirit as well. An easy way to understand this is to imagine the priorities in a husband's life. Of course God should be #1. Then, his spouse is #2, and then children are #3, and then work or personal hobbies probably falls into #4. Interestingly, because an oath to God is sworn for the sacrament of marriage, in some ways, a man's faithfulness to his spouse in the #2 position fulfills part of his obligation to God in the #1 position. Likewise, children, which come from the #2 spouse but are ranked #3 have a strong connection to the #2 spot. But, when push comes to shove, it is important to remember the order. Most marriages would continue on quite blissfully if each partner kept this order in their life. If you knock God off the #1 spot, it will be very hard to be faithful to your spouse or anyone else for that matter. If you keep God as #1 but move other things above your spouse, such as work, other people, or even the children, the marriage will struggle. Your spouse owns the #2 spot in your heart and anything that robs his/her spot violates the vow to faithfulness.

We are mostly talking about the ranking in one's heart and not necessarily a decision guide for every decision. For example, God should be #1, but you should not neglect your spouse and family to attend activities at the Church for 3 hours every night of the week. You might think you are keeping God as #1 but you might actually be putting "church activities" as opposed to God Himeslf above your spouse. People often struggle with putting their children about their spouses. In addition, while "work" and monetary gain should not take a place in your heart above your spouse, that does not mean you neglect supporting your spouse and family financially. Part of your commitment to your spouse is supporting him/her. You cannot use the above rankings to justify laziness or disorder in the heart.

A married Person's Priorities
1. **God**
2. **Spouse**
3. **Children**
4. **You pick**
5. **You pick**

Permanence

Permanence defines the length of time for which you will be united to your spouse, open to life, and faithful, and the definition of the length of time is......"until death do us part". A marriage lasts until one of the spouses dies. The marriage is dissolved at death and the surviving spouse is considered single and can remarry.

Contrary to some opinions, marriage cannot be ended by divorce. The oath that is sworn is "death do us part". Again, the Church does not impose this rule to limit the couple but rather reminds the couple of the binding oath they swore to one another.

When considering the commitment to fruitfulness, faithfulness, and permanence, one can become aware of the awesomeness of marriage and the gravity of the covenant. It can become a little more obvious why some men and women may choose to not marry and instead pursue a life of commitment to God alone. Nevertheless, the human desire for permanence finds its way in to even religious orders in which the members often make vows of commitment to the order for life.

Marriage as model of Christ's love for us

Marriage is a sign of Christ's love for us. When we consider how we would like Jesus to love us, we begin to see why the four elements of marriage must be in place. Marriage must involve faithfulness because we want Jesus to stay true to his promise to intercede for us to the Father and save us from our sins. We do not like to imagine a Jesus that changes his mind or that replaces us with a love for some other species in our place. Our covenant with God implies that he will stay faithful, which of course also means that His Covenant is permanent, like marriage. We also want God to be fruitful. We want and need the Holy Spirit to be poured out into our lives. We want the crucifixion to 'work', to do what it is supposed to do. Imagine if Jesus went through with the crucifixion but withheld his intention for the cruxifixion to give life. Imagine if the Father did not accept Jesus offering, his full gift of self. Our Christian Hope is based entirely on the fruitfulness, the life giving nature of Jesus sacrifice on the cross. We also expect the bread and wine to always become the body and blood of Jesus. We do not expect the priest to sometimes say the right prayers and sometimes not, leaving some of our communions to be with the body and blood of Jesus and other communions to be just a snack on bread and wine. We hold God to very high standards of unity, faithfulness, fruitfulness, and permanence. Marriage, which is his gift to us, is held to those same standards. Or, perhaps it is better to say that marriage, by definition, is those standards and anything else, cannot be called marriage.

Sacrament of Marriage

Sacrament	Marriage
Matter/Sign	consummation / life together
Words	Wedding Vows and a few key questions before the vows. 1) Oneness – sex and spiritual union 2) Fruitfulness –sexual acts are open to life 3) Faithfulness – only with each other 4) Permanence – until death
Minister	**Latin Rite:** Man and Woman exclusively **Eastern Rites**: Man, Woman, and Priest as witness
Graces	Receive Christ via Spouse (receptive emphasis) Grace to perfect love and holiness Children Image Trinity to the World

Marriage as a symbol of God's Love to Us

Spouse to Spouse	Marriage as image of God's love to Us
1. **Unity** physical and spiritual unity	1. **Unity:** - "I pray Father that they may be one as you and are one", Eucharist: Take this all of you and eat, this is my body, which will be given up for you".
2. **Fidelity** no adultery, spouse stays in no. 2 position in hearT	2. **Fidelity:** "You shall not have false Gods before me"
3. **Indissolubility** "until death do us part" no adultery	3. **Indissolubility:** eternal life w/ God. "nothing can separate us from the love of Christ"
4. **Fertility** openness to life, "no contraception"	4. **Fertility:** Holy Spirit creates new life within us.

When we see Marriage as a mirror or image that allows us to see and understand "how" God loves us, then we see that the four elements of marriage are very important and unchangeable. We might be tempted to desire that marriage does not have to forbid divorce, yet when we die, we expect the promise of the Father to save us through the son to still be available. We would be shocked to find that sometime between our death and our final judgment that Jesus and the Father got a divorce. We come to the gates of heaven ready to accept mercy through the sacrifice of the son, only to be told that that promise is no longer valid...it has ended. If this were possible, Christianity would have no "hope". In the same way, an idea of marriage that allows for the possibility of divorce lacks "hope". And, a marriage that keeps the vows and acknowledges all the vows give us a glimpse into the faithfulness of the Father and the Son.

One Guiding Principal – Several Conclusions

The guiding principle of sexual morality is that the sexual act is an expression of the four wedding vows or elements of marriage. A couple in high school that is not married should not engage sexually because they do not truly mean to say the four vows to one another. They are likely not open to life and they have not committed to one another for life. Their violation of the four elements of marriage is no different than a person engaging in homosexual activity. Homosexual activity cannot fulfill the fruitfulness requirement and therefore it is not in line with the principle that the sexual act is an expression of the four vows or four elements of marriage.

It is very important to distinguish in your mind between homosexual feelings and homosexual activity. If someone has feelings towards the same sex, these feelings, while not properly ordered, are not in and of themselves sinful. In the same way, it is easy for a non-married person to have heterosexual feelings towards the opposite sex. Again, these feelings are not wrong but acting on them or prolonging them on purpose would be wrong.

Similarly, a married man may find himself with feelings towards a woman that is not his wife. While the feelings may be somewhat initially out of his control, it is up to him to surrender the feelings to God and to avoid the near occasion of sin. The same could be said with someone who has feelings or emotions to hurt or even kill someone else. While these feelings may be natural or even somewhat justified, it is how the individual responds to the feelings that makes up the morality of the person's decision. In other words, in striving to live a moral life, we all face, at times, a difference between our feelings and what is the right thing to "do". Only by surrendering to God's healing power can we hope to ever have our feelings aligned with God's law.

Another tough conclusion of the one sexual guiding principal is the Church teaching on artificial insemination. Artificial insemination separates the love making act from conception and also violates the four vows. The sexual act is a physical way of saying the vows between the two people who are married. The doctor performing the insemination is not in the marriage. And, the means of creating the seeds for insemination would also have to have been done in violation of the vows of marriage. Once again, this can be a very sensitive topic. However, the teaching is a simple conclusion from the principle that the sexual act is a physical was of re-iterating the four vows. As such, the sexual act is the four vows and cannot violate the four vows. The Church does not take her positions on human sexuality from a standpoint of condemnation but rather from the standpoint of reminding the couple and all people what marriage is and what the four vows mean.

Compassion and Sensitivity

These tough teachings are natural extensions of the guiding principal that the sexual act is an expression of the four vows of marriage. However, people often struggle to obey these challenging mandates. As such, it is important to be charitable and merciful when discussing and teaching on these topics. On the one hand, the Church cannot change the logical extensions of the guiding sexual principal. On the other hand, the salvific act of Jesus Christ and his

80

love for humanity should probably be the first words out of our mouths to the world and to our friends. While never changing or backing down from the truth of these principles, we can be vigilant that our proclamation to the world is one of grace, mercy and forgiveness. It is much easier to help someone who knows and loves Jesus come to an understanding of the moral principles of sexuality than it is to convert someone to Jesus by only talking about sexual moral principles.

Questions

What did you learn in this chapter that you did not previously know?

Can you explain the means and ends chart?

From the charts, how does God's love for us demand fidelity?

What are the four elements of marriage?

Can you share a positive person story about being married? Or, a positive personal story about someone else's marriage if you are not married.

Pentecost, Prayer, and Ministry

The Power to live it out

We began with the spirit filled power of the proclamation of the Basic Gospel Message. Then, for most of the rest of the book we have been discussing rules, dogmas, codes, and beliefs. We've tried to make sense of all the "stuff" that Catholics believe and why they believe it. This content is very, very important. It is difficult to pray and live a moral life if your mind is mushy or confused on these moral and faith matters.

However, it is also very, very difficult to live out the above mentioned faith without God's help. At this point, you may be feeling a lot like the Apostles in the Upper room after the Ascension. Have you ever thought about how the Apostles were hanging out in that upper room scared? Think about it…why would they be scared? They had spent 3 full years with Jesus. They watched him preach, watched him heal, and watched him avoid most danger. Then, they watched him suffer, watched him die, saw him after his resurrection, spent some quality time with him on the beach, and then watched him ascend into heaven. The Apostles had the most complete take home guide to the Christian Faith available. They learned straight from the boss. They had the perfect retreat weekend. Yet, despite all their learning, all their studying with Jesus Himself, they were still afraid. The knowledge and even experience they had did not yet make sense. It did not yet lead to action. They didn't know or understand how they actually fit into the story itself. It was not until Pentecost that it all began to make sense to the Apostles.

I think we can feel like the Apostles all the time. We go to Church, we go to Catechism class, we take tests, we memorize the creed and our faith, yet we don't really "feel" different. We have learned that we are supposed to be God's chosen children, but, we feel pretty lost and confused. We will always feel this way until the Holy Spirit comes to visit us. The Holy Spirit is the great comforter. He is wisdom itself. He is also power, strength, and boldness. He is perfect language and perfect love. The Bible says we can't even say "Jesus is Lord" without the Holy Spirit.

Before Jesus ascended into heaven, he said "wait here and in a few days you will be baptized with the Holy Spirit". The Apostles probably did not know what he meant, but after Pentecost, they probably knew exactly what he meant. Baptized has its root in a Greek word, Baptizein, which means to immerse. So, Jesus was also saying, wait here and in a few days you will be immersed in the Holy Spirit.

At that first immersion, Pentecost, Peter stood up boldly and recounted much of salvation history very eloquently. It was as if Peter finally could understand and articulate the whole plan God had been working throughout history. Many were brought to faith that day and asked what to do. Peter said, "repent and be baptized for the forgiveness sins and you will receive the Holy Spirit". We too, if stirred by the gift of faith, ask Peter (The Church) what it is we can do in response to the gift of faith. The answer is the same, "repent and be baptized". Supposing we have already been baptized, then what? Unlike in the early Church in which the Basic Gospel Message, repenting, and being baptized where all rolled into one day long experience, we might have been baptized as a baby, accepted the Gospel in 3rd grade, and then still feel a bit out of the loop. We might very well be waiting for our personal Pentecost, which really isn't personal because it radically and quickly brings us into communion with God, the saints, and each other. But, from our subjective experience, we need a personal experience of Pentecost. We need to "know" and "feel" that everything we've been given by faith is real and worth acting on.

I encourage you to ask the Holy Spirit now to come into your life, to help you understand your Baptism and the forgiveness of sins that have been given to you. Ask him to make you bold and give you full understanding like he did to the Apostles at Pentecost. Ask him to help you be "baptized" in the Holy Spirit, to be "immersed" in the Holy Spirit. Remember the Holy Spirit descending on Jesus at his baptism in the Jordan by John. Now it is your turn to ask for and receive the Holy Spirit descending on you. If Jesus asked for the Holy Spirit at Baptism, it makes sense for you, a Christian, to do so too.

Many of the sacraments allow us to participate in the amazing grace that was given out in Jesus life. The Mass allows us to be present at the cross when Jesus gave himself for us to the Father. Holy Orders makes present Jesus choosing of the Apostles and institution of the priesthood at the Last Supper. And Baptism and Confirmation make present for us the power and grace of Pentecost. We cannot say Jesus is Lord without the Holy Spirit and thus it is very unlikely anything written above in this book will make sense, at least meaningful sense, without the Holy Spirit.

I encourage you to read the first five chapters of Acts of the Apostles. Observe the changes the Apostles go through personally and in their ministry. Then, ask the Holy Spirit for an outpouring of the same exact grace in your life. Don't be afraid. Everything that happened in the Acts of the Apostles still happens to day. It would probably happen a lot more if we dared to ask.

St. Paul says in Romans, "We do not know how to pray as we ought, but the Spirit intercedes on behalf with groanings too deep for human words to understand, but the Father who searches all hearts understands."

I love, love, love this verse because if Saint Paul didn't know how to pray, why should I figure I know how to pray? I love coming to prayer time and saying to God.. "umm, excuse me, but Saint Paul said I didn't know how to pray but that you might be sending the Holy Spirit to intercede for me…can I have some of the Holy Spirit please?". Of course, then I feel great because I'm reminded of something else Jesus said, "If an evil earthly father would not give his son a snake when he asks for bread, how much more will your Father in heaven, who is Good, give you the Holy Spirit when you ask". So, asking for the Holy Spirit seems to be a normative part of communicating with God.

I also like to ask for the Holy Spirit because it is a prayer I'm pretty sure will get answered. I unfortunately cannot share you with the secret of how to pray for a Lamborghini and have it appear…believe me I'm working on it. But, as of yet, I haven't unlocked the mystery of getting that prayer request answered. However, it does seem that almost every time we ask for the Holy Spirit, it is given. Think of it like stepping closer to the basketball hoop to make some easy baskets to build your confidence. Just ask for the Holy Spirit if you want to have some prayers answered. But, be warned, the Holy Spirit is the greatest gift and you might find after receiving Him that you that you either don't need to be taking those long shots anymore, or you'll figure out how to ask for them in better ways.

Service and Charisms

Jesus says some very strong words about serving those in need. He even warns us that He may not recognize us if we call on his name but have never served him in those in need. As we look at the world, we can find a lot of situations of need. It can be overwhelming. But, the Holy Spirit of Pentecost has guidance for us. Recall that immediately after Pentecost, Peter is approached by a crippled man who asks Peter for money. Peter replies, "Silver and Gold I do not have, but what I do have I give you. In the name of Jesus of Nazareth get up and walk". The man is immediately healed. Peter received special gifts at Pentecost to allow him to do ministry like Jesus did. A careful reader would observe that while Jesus is no longer in the story in his bodily form, Peter and the Apostles seem to be "doing" everything Jesus was doing. Jesus ministry has carried on.

You will likely find the most peace and blessing in your service and ministry by asking the Holy Spirit to show you in which ways you have been gifted. These special gifts of service are called charisms. They are not talents or dispositions you might discover from a personality test. Rather, they are an anointing the Holy Spirit places upon you and a particular type of service. When you use a charism the person you are serving feels as if they are encountering God himself. God is working through you. Imagine going to serve food to a homeless person and receiving an anointed guidance to pray for that person. Imagine if through your prayer, the Holy Spirit removes an addiction or other cause of pain and suffering from the homeless person. It could be that the addiction or other ailment was the primary reason that person was homeless. With the ailment removed, the person may move onto a permanent path of recovery and self-sufficiency. Jesus seemed to constantly be healing crippled and blind people who were dependent on almsgiving to live. He was setting them free spiritually and physically. Our ministry and service does not need to be limited to the physical world, as Christians, we bring to the act of service something supernatural. We bring faith and healing in the name of Jesus Christ. Now, of course, we don't necessarily see a miraculous healing every time we pray for it. However, we see it enough times that it makes praying every time worth it. If you found that 1 out of 10 people you prayed for received instantly healing, you would see a lot more healings if you prayed for 100 people per week. If you've only ever prayed for 5 people in your life, how can you be so sure you don't have a charism of healing? And, many times someone does receive a blessing that begins a chain of events that leads to at least the type of healing that person received. Many times people do not tell you what they felt or received when you prayed for them. They me be embarrassed or surprised. You have to trust that you did your part and God did His.

Even if your area of service is something like teaching the faith, you can pray before your teaching that it will bear fruit. You may not have everyone in the audience come and clearly tell you that they experienced God in a major way during your talk. But, if you are gifted in teaching, it is most likely the case that someone did. Recall that Jesus spent time with a lot of people whose hearts he could not win. In fact, it seems the people he spent the most time with outside of his apostles, ended up putting him to death. So, just remember that everyone has a free will and even if you help them to see God, they are still free to respond how they wish.

Here is a common list of charisms or gifts of service. Pray while reading this list and see if any of the gifts stand out. Also, read more about and experiment serving in some of these areas. You may have a special gift waiting to be uncovered. Remember, they are not necessarily the same as talents or skills you have built.

Encouragement
Hospitality
Pastoring
Helping
Mercy
Administration
Leadership
Giving
Service
Evangalism
Prophecy
Teaching
Healing
Intercessory Prayer
Knowledge
Wisdom
Discernment of Spirits
Craftsmanship
Writing
Music
Celibacy
Voluntary Poverty
Missionary
Faith

Questions

Do you ever have a hard time getting excited about your faith?

Would something like a personal Pentecost help you?

Are you a little bit afraid of experiencing power and strength from the Holy Spirit?

Do you know anyone that you think is truly living in the grace of Pentecost?

Do you have a sense that God has something more for you?

In what area do you feel most inclined to serve those in need?

Can you share a personal story of when you used a gift or charism for ministry?

Can you share a personal story of when you were on the receiving end of someone else's charism.

Contact the Author

Michael Tigue
mtigue@web4uonline.com
888-254-3213

Made in the USA
Monee, IL
25 October 2022